Chords in A natural minor scale

	Am i	Bdim ii°	C III	Dm iv	Em v	F VI	G VII
I	Am	Bdim	C	Dm	Em	F	G
II		Bdim					
III			C 3 fr			F 3 fr	G 3 fr
IV					Em 4 fr		
V	Am 5 fr		C 5 fr	Dm 5 fr		F 5 fr	G 5 fr
VI		Bdim 6 fr					
VII	Am 7 fr	Bdim 7 fr		Dm 7 fr	Em 7 fr		G 7 fr
VIII			C 8 fr			F 8 fr	
IX	Am 9 fr	Bdim 9 fr			Em 9 fr		
X				Dm 10 fr		F 10 fr	G 10 fr
XI							

Chords in E natural minor scale (Em)

	Em i	F#dim ii°	G III	Am iv	Bm v	C VI	D VII
I							
II							
III							
IV							
V							
VI							
VII							
VIII							
IX							
X							
XI							

Chords in D natural minor scale (Dm)

	Dm i	Edim ii°	F III	Gm iv	Am v	Bb VI	C VII
I	Dm	Edim	F	Gm	Am	Bb	C
II		Edim					
III			F (3 fr)	Gm (3 fr)		Bb (3 fr)	C (3 fr)
IV							
V	Dm (5 fr)		F (5 fr)	Gm (5 fr)	Am (5 fr)		C (5 fr)
VI		Edim (6 fr)				Bb (6 fr)	
VII	Dm (7 fr)	Edim (7 fr)		Gm (7 fr)	Am (7 fr)		
VIII			F (8 fr)			Bb (8 fr)	C (8 fr)
IX					Am (9 fr)		
X	Dm (10 fr)		F (10 fr)	Gm (10 fr)		Bb (10 fr)	
XI		Edim (11 fr)					

Chords in G natural minor scale (Gm)

	Gm i	Adim ii°	Bb III	Cm iv	Dm v	Eb VI	F VII
I	Gm	Adim	Bb	Cm	Dm	Eb	F
II							
III	Gm		Bb	Cm		Eb	F
IV		Adim 4 fr					
V	Gm 5 fr	Adim 5 fr		Cm 5 fr	Dm 5 fr		F 5 fr
VI			Bb 6 fr			Eb 6 fr	
VII	Gm 7 fr	Adim 7 fr			Dm 7 fr		
VIII			Bb 8 fr	Cm 8 fr		Eb 8 fr	F 8 fr
IX							
X	Gm 10 fr		Bb 10 fr	Cm 10 fr	Dm 10 fr		F 10 fr
XI		Adim 11 fr				Eb 11 fr	

Chords in B natural minor scale (Bm)

	Bm i	C#dim ii°	D III	Em iv	F#m v	G VI	A VII
I							
II							
III							
IV							
V							
VI							
VII							
VIII							
IX							
X							
XI							

Chords in F natural minor scale (Fm)

	Fm i	Gdim ii°	Ab III	Bbm iv	Cm v	Db VI	Eb VII
I	Fm		Ab	Bbm	Cm	Db	Eb
II		Gdim					
III	Fm 3 fr	Gdim 3 fr		Bbm 3 fr	Cm 3 fr		Eb 3 fr
IV			Ab 4 fr			Db 4 fr	
V	Fm 5 fr	Gdim 5 fr			Cm 5 fr		
VI			Ab 6 fr	Bbm 6 fr		Db 6 fr	Eb 6 fr
VII							
VIII	Fm 8 fr		Ab 8 fr	Bbm 8 fr	Cm 8 fr		Eb 8 fr
IX		Gdim 9 fr				Db 9 fr	
X	Fm 10 fr	Gdim 10 fr		Bbm 10 fr	Cm 10 fr		
XI			Ab 11 fr			Db 11 fr	Eb 11 fr

Chords in C natural minor scale (Cm)

	Cm i	Ddim ii°	Eb III	Fm iv	Gm v	Ab VI	Bb VII
I	Cm	Ddim	Eb	Fm	Gm	Ab	Bb
II							
III	Cm 3 fr		Eb 3 fr	Fm 3 fr	Gm 3 fr		Bb 3 fr
IV		Ddim 4 fr				Ab 4 fr	
V	Cm 5 fr	Ddim 5 fr		Fm 5 fr	Gm 5 fr		
VI			Eb 6 fr			Ab 6 fr	Bb 6 fr
VII					Gm 7 fr		
VIII	Cm 8 fr		Eb 8 fr	Fm 8 fr		Ab 8 fr	Bb 8 fr
IX		Ddim 9 fr					
X	Cm 10 fr	Ddim 10 fr		Fm 10 fr	Gm 10 fr		Bb 10 fr
XI			Eb 11 fr			Ab 11 fr	

All Chords in Minor Progressions

i	ii°	III	iv	v	VI	VII
Am	Bdim	C	Dm	Em	F	G
Bm	C#dim	D	Em	F#m	G	A
Cm	Ddim	Eb	Fm	Gm	Ab	Bb
Dm	Edim	F	Gm	Am	Bb	C
Em	F#dim	G	Am	Bm	C	D
Fm	Gdim	Ab	Bbm	Cm	Db	Eb
Gm	Adim	Bb	Cm	Dm	Eb	F

The table below says the next: Chord Am is iv in Em tonality and v in Dm tonality.
Chord Gm is i in Gm tonality, iv in Dm tonality and also is v in the Cm.

	i	ii°	III	iv	v	VI	VII
Am	Am			Em	Dm		
Bbm				Fm			
Bm	Bm				Em		
Cm	Cm			Gm	Fm		
Dm	Dm			Am	Gm		
Em	Em			Bm	Am		
Fm	Fm			Cm			
F#m							
Gm	Gm			Dm	Cm		
Ab			Am			Em	
A							Bm
Bb						Dm	Cm
C						Em	Dm
Db						Fm	
D			Bm				Em
Eb			Cm			Gm	
F			Dm			Am	Gm
G			Em			Dm	Am
Adim		Gm					
Bdim		Am					
C#dim		Bm					
Ddim		Cm					
Edim		Dm					
F#dim		Em					
Gdim		Fm					

Chords in C major scale (C)

	C I	Dm ii	Em iii	F IV	G V	Am vii	Bdim vii°
I	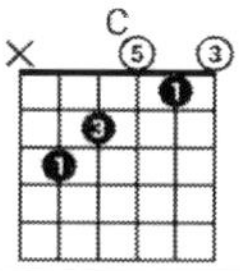	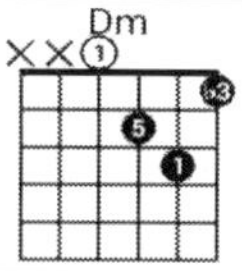	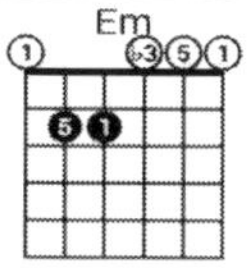	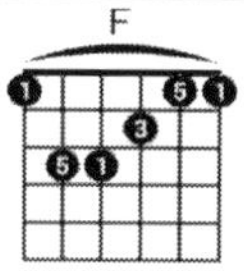	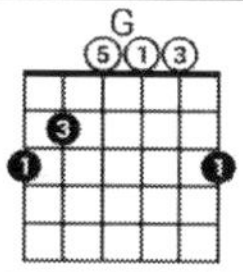	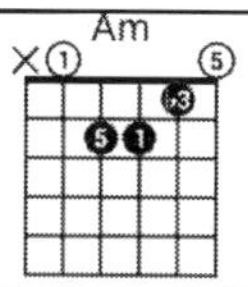	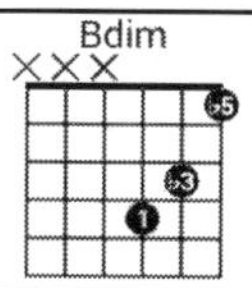
II							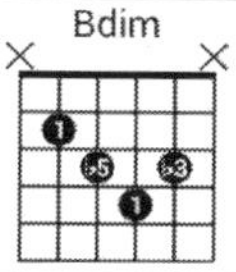
III	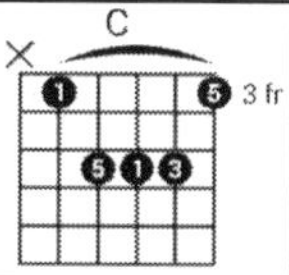			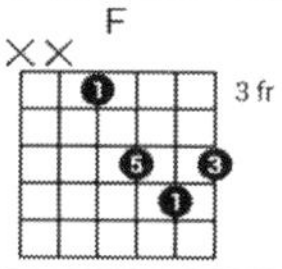	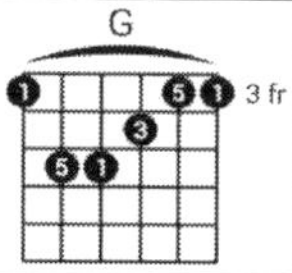		
IV			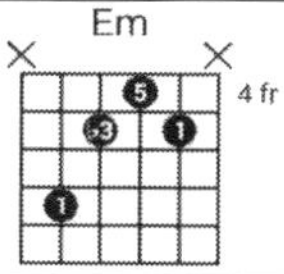				
V	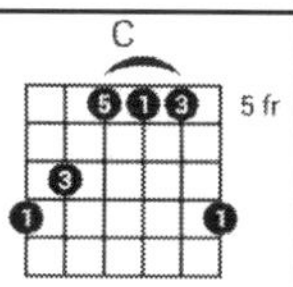	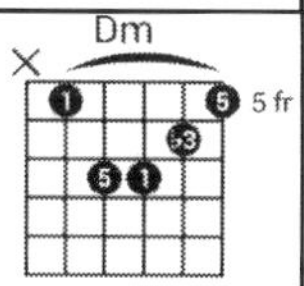		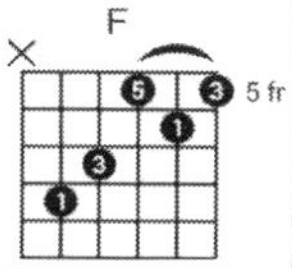	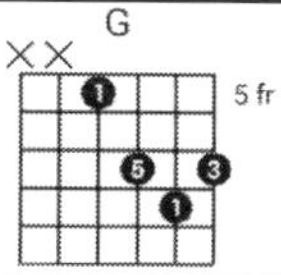	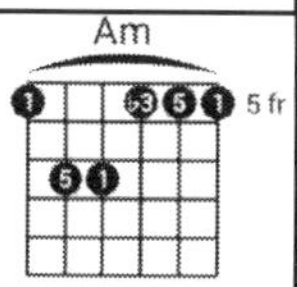	
VI							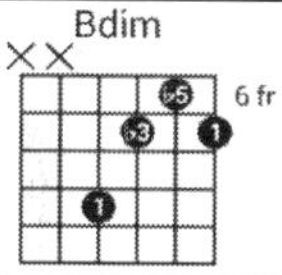
VII		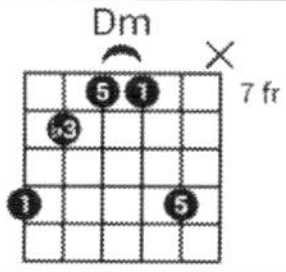	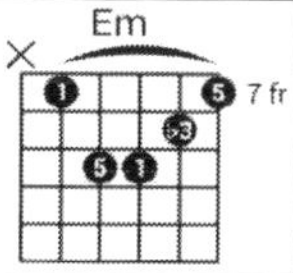		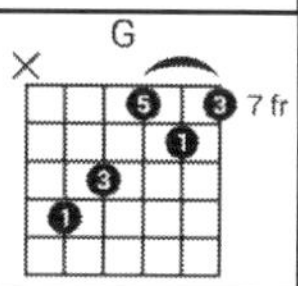	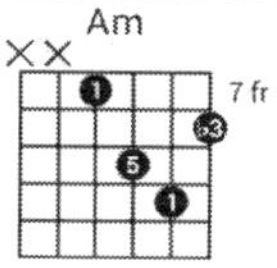	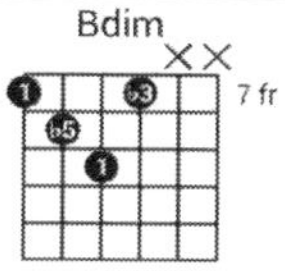
VIII	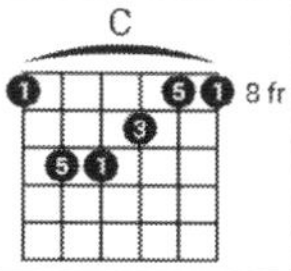			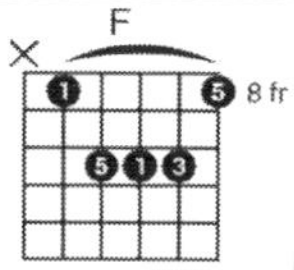			
IX			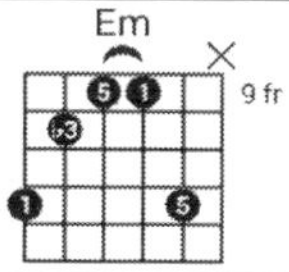			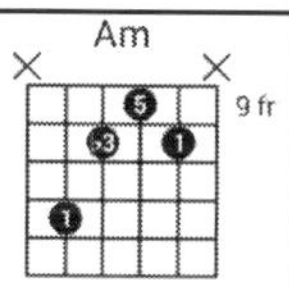	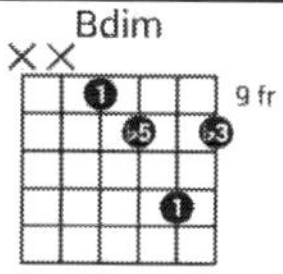
X		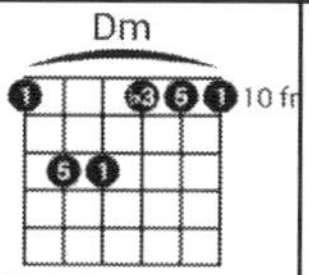		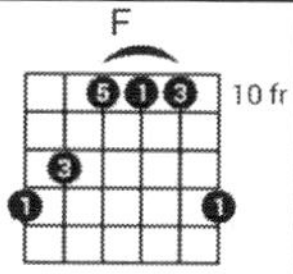	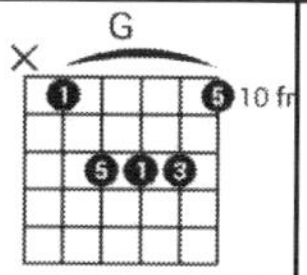		
XI							

Chords in F major scale (F)

Chords in G major scale (G)

	G I	Am ii	Bm iii	C IV	D V	Em vii	F#dim vii°
I							
II							
III							
IV							
V							
VI							
VII							
VIII							
IX							
X							
XI							

Chords in D major scale (D)

	D I	Em ii	F#m iii	G IV	A V	Bm vii	C#dim vii°
I		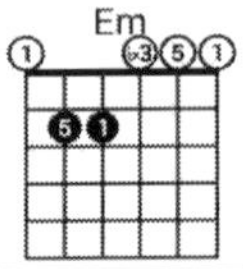		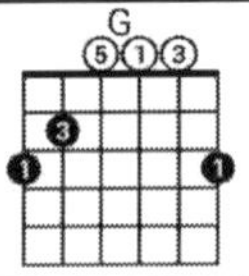			
II	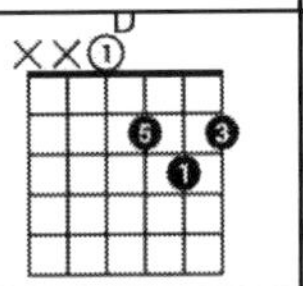		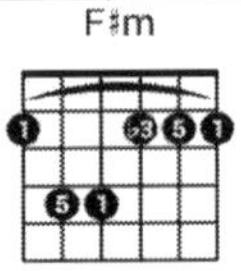		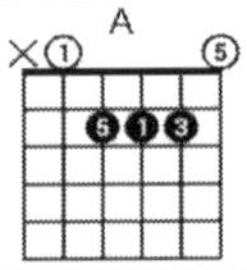	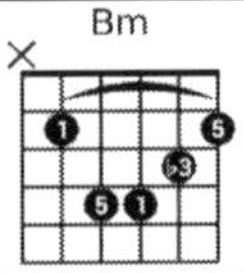	
III				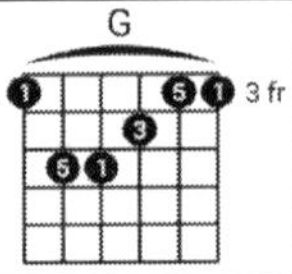			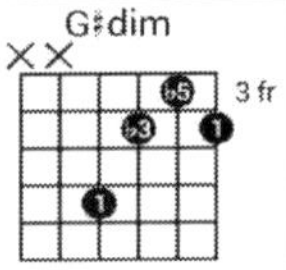
IV		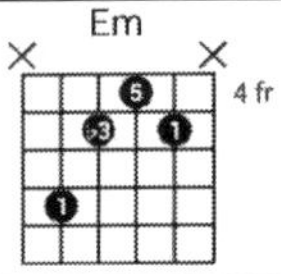	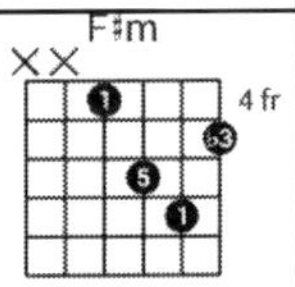			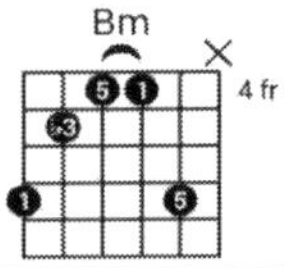	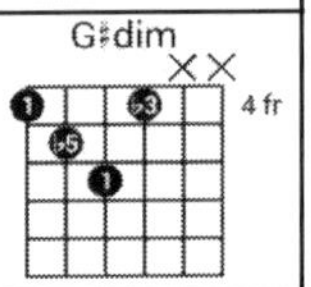
V	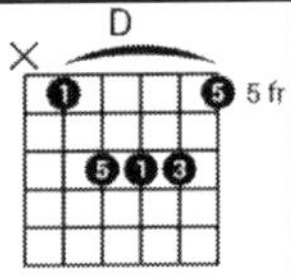			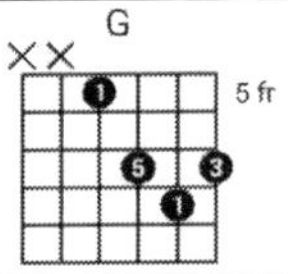	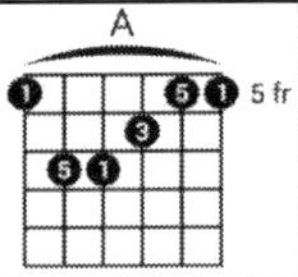		
VI			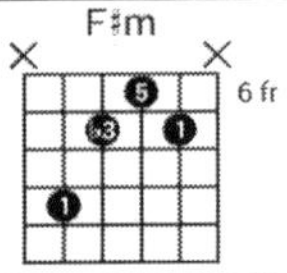				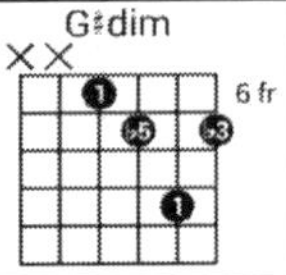
VII	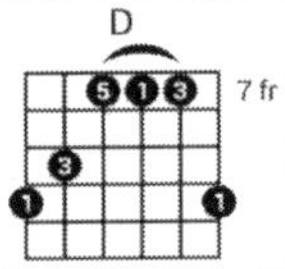	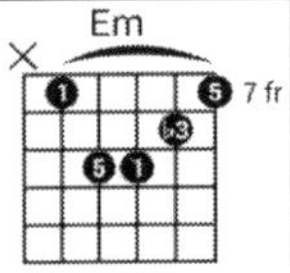		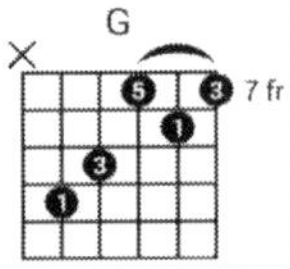	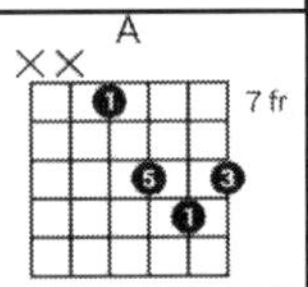	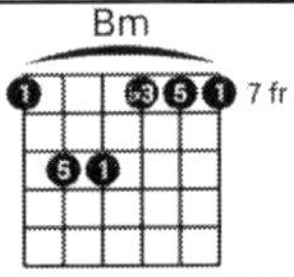	
VIII							
IX		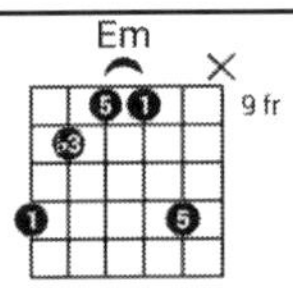	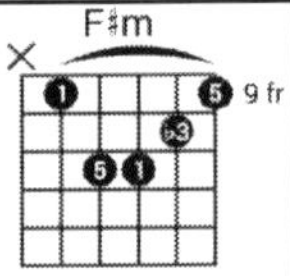		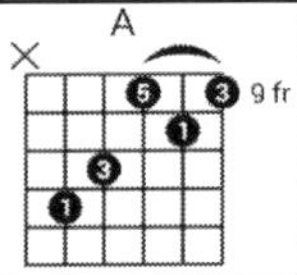	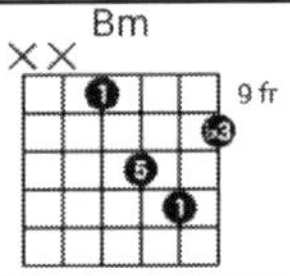	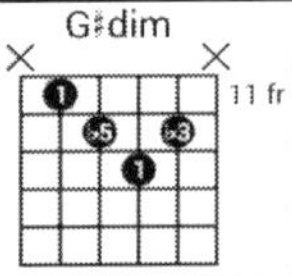
X	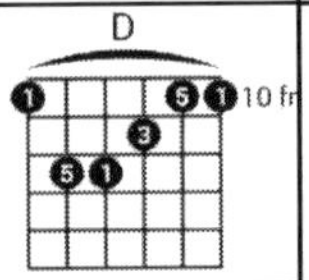			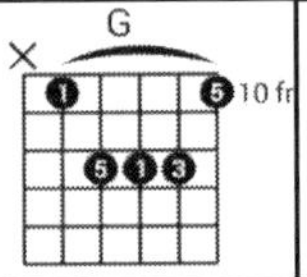			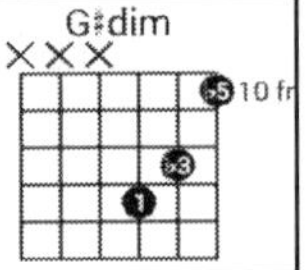
XI			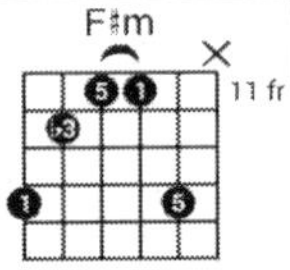				

Chords in A major scale (A)

	A I	Bm ii	C#m iii	D IV	E V	F#m vii	G#dim vii°
I			C#m		E		
II	A	Bm		D	E	F#m	
III							G#dim
IV		Bm	C#m		E	F#m	G#dim
V	A			D			
VI			C#m			F#m	G#dim
VII	A	Bm		D	E		
VIII							
IX	A	Bm	C#m		E	F#m	G#dim
X				D			G#dim
XI						F#m	

13

Chords in E major scale (E)

	E I	F#m ii	G#m iii	A IV	B V	C#m vii	D#dim vii°
I							
II							
III							
IV							
V							
VI							
VII							
VIII							
IX							
X							
XI							

14

Chords in B major scale (B)

	B i	C#m ii	D#m iii	E IV	F# V	G#m vii	A#dim vii°
I		C#m	C#m	E		G#m	A#dim
II	B			E	F#		
III							
IV	B	C#m	C#m	E	F#	G#m	
V							A#dim
VI		C#m	C#m		F#	G#m	A#dim
VII	B			E			
VIII						G#m	A#dim
IX	B	C#m	C#m	E	F#		
X							
XI	B				F#	G#m	

15

All Chords in Major Progressions

I	ii	iii	IV	V	vi	vii°
A	Bm	C#m	D	E	F#m	G#dim
B	C#m	D#m	E	F#	G#m	A#dim
C	Dm	Em	F	G	Am	Bdim
D	Em	F#m	G	A	Bm	C#dim
E	F#m	G#m	A	B	C#m	D#dim
F	Gm	Am	Bb	C	Dm	Edim
G	Am	Bm	C	D	Em	F#dim

And the similar view of the Major chords belong to the degree of tonalities

	I	ii	iii	IV	V	vi	vii°
A	A			E	D		
Bb				F			
B	B				E		
C	C			G	F		
D	D			A	G		
E	E			B	A		
F	F			C			
F#					B		
G	G			D	C		
Am		G	F	C			
Bm		A	G			D	
C#m		B	A			E	
Dm		C				F	
D#m			B				
Em		D	C			G	
F#m		E	D			A	
Gm		F					
G#m			E			B	
A#dim							B
Bdim							C
C#dim							D
D#dim							E
Edim							F
F#dim							G
G#dim							A

Fretboard diagram A natural minor scale (Am)

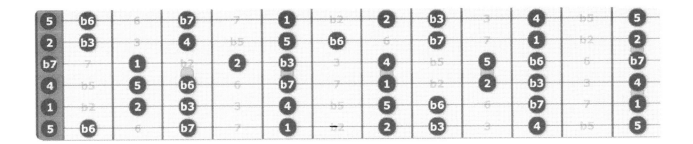

Fretboard diagram E natural minor scale (Em)

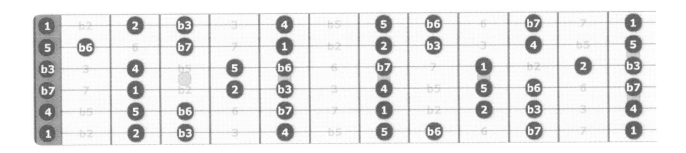

Fretboard diagram D natural minor scale (Dm)

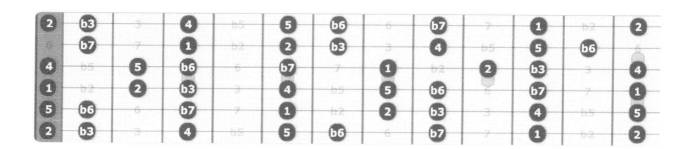

Fretboard diagram G natural minor scale (Gm)

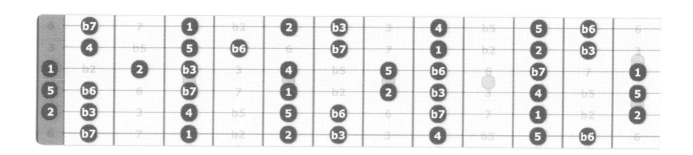

Fretboard diagram B natural minor scale (Bm)

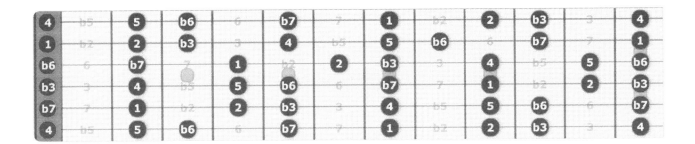

Fretboard diagram F natural minor scale (Fm)

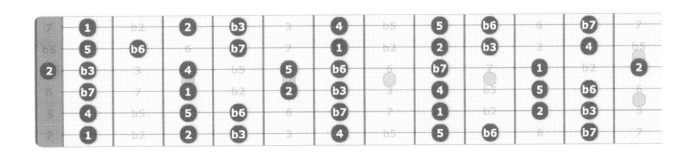

Fretboard diagram C natural minor scale (Cm)

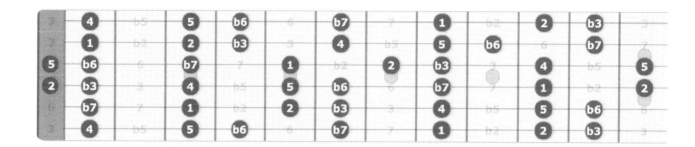

Fretboard diagram C major scale (C)

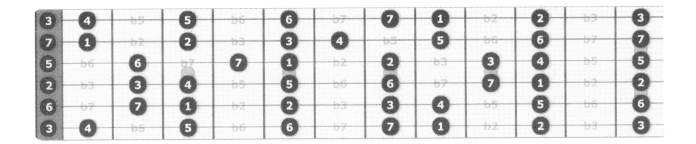

Fretboard diagram F major scale (F)

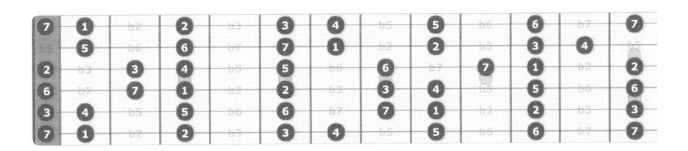

Fretboard diagram G major scale (G)

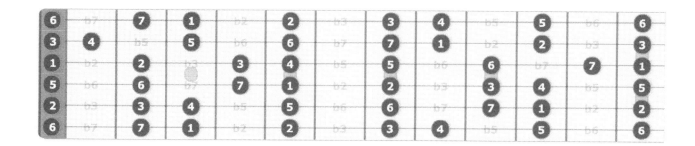

Fretboard diagram D major scale (D)

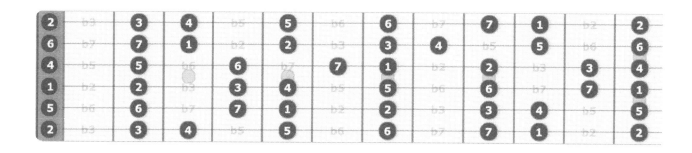

Fretboard diagram A major scale (A)

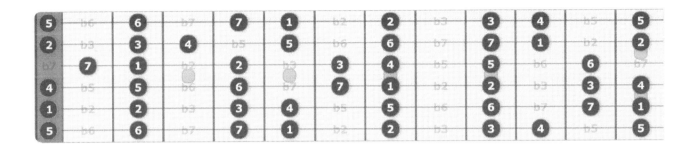

Fretboard diagram E major scale (E)

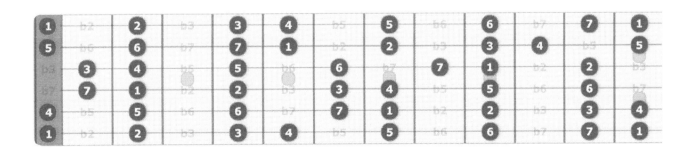

Fretboard diagram B major scale (B)

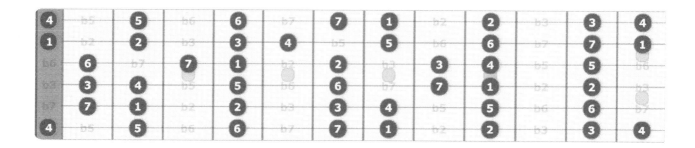

About

How to play Chord progressions without jumping across the fretboard? Where are second-degree chords in Em?
Where is G chord first-degree bass note of the 5th string?

And many similar questions when you begin learning the fretboard. This book is for the guitarists, songwriters, and instructors to help with the chord progressions visualization on the fretboard. Each table: Chord Shape->Progression Degree->Fretboard position.

In addition, there is the interesting table view of Minor and Major chords belong to the degree of tonalities.

For all tonalities, I've added fretboard diagrams to support the quick navigation across the neck.

Visit https://guitarillaz.blogspot.com/ for more information about guitars, gear, lessons, software and apps for musicians.

Contents

Printed in Great Britain
by Amazon